WRONGLY CHARGED WITH A DWI IN TEXAS?

Fight The Unfair Charges And Reclaim Your Life!

MARK DIAZ, ESQ.
THOMAS OVERHOUSE, ESQ.

Jacobs & Whitehall
73-03 Bell Blvd, #10
Oakland Gardens, NY 11364
www.jacobsandwhitehall.com

Ordering Information:

Quantity sales. Special discounts are available on quantity purchases by corporations, associations, and others. For details, contact the publisher at the address above.

Orders by U.S. trade bookstores and wholesalers. Please contact Jacobs & Whitehall: Tel: (888) 991-2766 or visit www.jacobsandwhitehall.com.

Printed in the United States of America

Published in 2021

ISBN: 978-1-951149-64-2

PREFACE

Our primary practice area is in Galveston County, Texas. While we regularly handle cases in Harris County, Brazoria County, and others; our viewpoint mainly comes from cases in Galveston County. Additionally, we focus on criminal defense of felonies and misdemeanors, most of the information in this book does not apply to Class C Misdemeanors.

While we also handle Federal Criminal Defense, this short booklet deals only with the Defense of cases in State/County Court and not Federal cases. While the basic principles of the jury trial, rights, consequences, and role of the Attorney may be similar; punishment and plea bargaining are completely different.

Of course, with all the information available on the internet today, most of the information here in our little publication can be found browsing the internet. This is meant to be a helpful quick read to answer simple questions and help start the process if you have found yourself in the unfortunate position of facing criminal charges. It also gives some insight into the way we try to interact with our clients.

DEDICATION

We would like to dedicate this book to all of our past, current, and future clients.

Also, Matthew Sloan, a previous associate at the firm. Matt was taken from us too early when he tragically perished in an automobile accident on May 13, 2020.

DISCLAIMER

This publication is intended to be used for educational purposes only. No legal advice is being given, and no attorney-client relationship is intended to be created by reading this material. The author assumes no liability for any errors or omissions or for how this book or its contents are used or interpreted, or for any consequences resulting directly or indirectly from the use of this book. For legal or any other advice, please consult an experienced attorney or the appropriate expert, who is aware of the specific facts of your case and is knowledgeable in the law in your jurisdiction.

Mark Diaz Attorney at Law

719 59th St
Galveston, TX 77551
(409) 515-6170
www.texascriminaljustice.com

TESTIMONIALS

"I hired Katy Jo Muncie with the Diaz firm who handled the lead on my 2 DWI charges in different counties. Along with Mark Diaz, Katy Jo was there for me every step of the way. After firing my first attorney, I was very nervous about what my outcome would be. Katy Jo was patient and worked the system ultimately getting, what in my opinion, was the best outcome for me in the cases. These cases involved a lot of multiple D.A.s and judges, different counties and courts, Texas DPS, etc. I would highly recommend the services of these two fine people. You will be treated with respect and can have the confidence that they know the people and have the experience to get the best outcome. Thank you, Katy Jo."

– David

****

"Throughout my trials, Mark Diaz and Katy Jo Muncie worked side by side and handled my case with ease. Aside from initiating my first consultation over the phone and making my appearances to court, I held zero responsibility throughout the process. When my case was settled, my DWI charge was reduced to Obstruction of Highway, and I blew double the legal alcohol limit for my BAC test. I will definitely recommend Mark or Katy Jo if anyone I know needs an attorney in the future."

– Martin

****

"I have hired Mark on a number of occasions. He is very communicative which is important to me in these situations. He is honest and gives you all the information you need to make an informed decision. I highly recommend Mark and use him exclusively when I require these types of services. I have always had great results when using Mark."

– Alva

****

"Highly recommend Mr. Diaz. His confidence in his ability to have a lawsuit against us dismissed gave us peace of mind during a stressful time. It was not a matter of IF he would win it was just a matter of WHEN. He handily defeated the opposing council in one court appearance. Very thankful to have had him on our side."

– Anonymous

****

TABLE OF CONTENTS

About The Authors

MARK DIAZ

I've been practicing law for over two decades, since 1998. I started trying DWI cases before blood tests, breath tests, and dash or body cameras were available.

Mark Diaz has been aggressively defending the rights of Texans for more than twenty years. A 1998 graduate of Thurgood Marshall School of Law who obtained his undergraduate degree from the University of Houston, Mark concentrates his practice solely in the area of criminal defense. He is admitted to practice law in all Texas state courts as well as federal court in the United States District Court for the

Southern District of Texas. Mark is a seasoned trial lawyer who has tried every kind of criminal case.

Mark lives on the island and is often in the community at local events. It is not unusual for him to run into clients, both present and past while out and about on the island. Along with his wife Kristie, they are raising two children, so they are often at sports events or local youth events. Living in the community also allows Mark to meet clients at the office during off hours and sometimes over the weekend.

Mark prides himself on his ability to quickly respond to the needs and concerns of his clients.

My associate, Thomas Overhouse, became a licensed attorney in 2016 and began working for me after spending almost four years at the Galveston County District Attorney's Office. During his time there, he handled hundreds if not thousands of DWI cases and took many of those cases to trial. Within one year, he was promoted to a felony prosecutor and ultimately became a senior felony prosecutor. Thomas continues to attend various specialized DWI courses on the DWI defense.

THOMAS OVERHOUSE

In 2012, Thomas graduated suma cum laude from the University of St. Thomas with a Bachelor of Arts in History. Upon completion of his undergraduate degree, Thomas attended South Texas College of Law and earned his law degree. Additionally, Thomas is a certified a Field Sobreity Test Practitioner through the police academy offered at College of the Mainland.

Thomas began his legal career as an Assistant District Attorney in the Misdemeanor Division of the Galveston County District Attorney's Office. In his first year, Thomas managed large misdemeanor dockets consisting of a wide array of different misdemeanor charges and often tried them to a jury.

After his first year, Thomas began to rise through the ranks and was promoted into the Felony Trial Bureau, ultimately earning the position of Senior Felony Prosecutor. While in the Felony Trial Bureau, Thomas handled hundreds of cases and conducted many jury trials of all levels of felonies in the 10th, 56th, 212th, and 405th Judicial District Courts.

Thomas' time as a prosecutor taught him how to analyze a criminal case for strengths and weaknesses and gained inside information about the operation of law enforcement. He took great pride in taking difficult cases to trial by jury and overcoming the challenges they presented. Thomas is taking the skills and experience he gained at the District Attorney's Office to now assist those who have been accused of a crime.

He understands that underneath the accusation there is a person who just needs help. Thomas is committed to applying his knowledge of how the prosecution thinks and operates to benefit those who have been accused and ensure that they receive the justice they so truly deserve.

CHAPTER 1

HOW IS DWI DEFINED UNDER TEXAS STATE LAW?

Driving While Intoxicated, or DWI is an offense under the Texas Penal Code and is defined as operating a motor vehicle in a public place while intoxicated. The Penal Code further defines *intoxicated* in two alternative ways:

1) an individual not having the normal use of their physical or mental faculties by the

introduction of alcohol, drug, or a combination of both into the body;

2) an individual with a blood alcohol concentration of 0.08 or more.

Although DWI and DUI are often used interchangeably to mean the same thing; they are two different offenses with key distinctions. A DUI, or Driving Under the Influence, is actually an offense under the Texas Transportation Code. It is charged when an individual under the age of 21 is accused of operating a motor vehicle with *any* detectable amount of alcohol in their system. Hence the inclusion of the term "influence" in the title instead of "intoxicated". However, it should be noted that an individual under the age of 21 can still be charged with a DWI if they meet the Penal Code's definition of intoxicated.

What Happens When Someone Is Pulled Over For Suspicion Of DWI?

First, it is imperative to understand that an officer has already begun investigating and collecting evidence even before someone has been pulled over for suspicion of DWI. For instance, most DWI related traffic stops occur after an officer observed certain driving behaviors or traffic violations. These observations are typically captured on video by a camera mounted inside of the officer's patrol vehicle. This video evidence can be used to bolster the State's prosecution of a DWI, but it can also reveal legal issues that are harmful to the State's case.

After an officer initiates a traffic stop for suspicion of DWI, the officer will approach the vehicle, make contact with the driver, and indicate the reason for the stop. The officer's primary goal at this point is to begin a preliminary investigation to obtain incriminating evidence or statements from the driver. The officer is looking for any signs of intoxication, e.g. odor of alcohol, slurred speech, bloodshot eyes, poor motor skills, etc. Remember, the camera is still recording both video and audio of this interaction. One officer has told us in the past that his whole purpose at this time is to try to get the driver to talk as much as possible in order to obtain evidence.

If the officer believes he has observed enough initial signs, he will then ask the driver to step out of the vehicle and move to a spot within view of the in-car camera. Fully aware that this entire interaction is still being recorded, the officer will ask the driver more questions with the hope that the camera will record additional self-incriminating statements or other signs of intoxication such as stumbling or swaying.

Once the officer believes enough preliminary evidence has been collected, the driver will then be instructed to perform a battery of roadside tests called standardized field sobriety tests (SFSTs). An officer may not tell a driver that participation in the SFSTs is not mandatory, therefore a driver may be unaware of the fact that they have the right to refuse to take any of the tests.

As previously mentioned, I was fortunate to be invited to attend the Standardized Field Sobriety Test Practitioner portion of the police academy at College of the Mainland. In this course, I received the actual training and instruction that police officers undergo taught by leading law enforcement experts in Galveston County. Ultimately, I received the exact knowledge and inside tips of the trade that officers are equipped with and earned my certification as an SFST practitioner.

COM

LAW ENFORCEMENT TRAINING CENTER #511264

Texas City, Texas

Thomas Blair Overhouse

Standardized Field Sobriety Test

CERTIFICATE of COMPLETION

SFSTs are comprised of a battery of three separate tests: the HGN test, the Walk and Turn, and the One Leg Stand. These are designed to induce the subject to exhibit what are referred to by officers as "clues". Officers will often testify that SFSTs are not pass or fail tests, but rather tests looking for any indicators of intoxication, or "clues". The distinction between "clue" and pass or fail is nothing more than clever world play that officers are taught to use in their training. One must understand that the presence of enough "clues" is the functional equivalent of a failure and is likely to lead to an arrest for DWI. Although SFSTs are based on science, they are far from perfect and in many ways flawed. An attorney with the right knowledge and experience can help someone take advantage of the subtle, yet significant, flaws when building a criminal defense.

The first test administered is the horizontal gaze nystagmus (HGN) test, commonly referred to as the "eye test". This test is designed to detect nystagmus, which is an involuntary jerking of the eye that can be caused by the consumption of alcohol or certain drugs. The HGN test is conducted by asking the subject to follow a stimulus, often a penlight, back and forth with their eyes. This particular test is comprised of three phases each designed to show clues of intoxication. However, some head injuries or other medical conditions can cause the presence of nystagmus, which would disqualify someone as a candidate for taking the HGN test.

Once the officer has determined that the driver is a proper candidate for HGN, the officer will move on to the phases of the test. The first phase is designed to detect a lack of smooth pursuit, or in other words, whether each eye tracks the stimulus smoothly. In the second phase, the officer asks the subject to follow the stimulus with their eyes to a point referred to as maximum deviation (eyes fully looking to the corner) trying to detect the presence of nystagmus. During the third and last phase, the officer asks the subject to follow the stimulus with their eyes again and looks for the presence of nystagmus prior to the stimulus being at approximately 45 degrees off the side of the face.

The presence of any nystagmus will be considered a "clue" indicating possible intoxication. Although the presence of any nystagmus in the subject's eye is entirely involuntary, any observations of it are very subjective to the observer and are rarely captured on video.

The second test in the SFST battery is the "walk-and-turn", which requires the subject to maneuver into the "starting position" and remain there during the instruction phase. The subject will be instructed to take nine heel-to-toe steps, with their arms at their side while counting the number of steps out loud along an imaginary straight line. The officer will then explain that once the person has reached the ninth step, they must take a series of small steps while turning around and then take nine steps back in the same manner as the first nine steps.

Sound confusing? That is because it is designed to be. This type of test is named a divided attention test and is designed to test the taker's ability to recall and follow the instructions while performing the physical tasks. Fail to follow any of the instructions precisely and it will be held against you. As one might imagine, this is a very unnatural exercise and can be quite difficult regardless of whether someone has consumed any alcohol or drugs.

The third standardized field sobriety test that will be conducted is the one-leg-stand. The officer will ask the subject to get into the same "starting position" and remain there during the instructions. The officer will then instruct the subject to pick whichever leg they are more comfortable with, raise their foot approximately six inches off of the ground while keeping the toe pointed outward, and count out loud, "one thousand one, one thousand two" and so on until the officer instructs the driver to stop. The duration of this test is entirely at the officer's discretion but should last no longer than 30 seconds. Again, fail to follow any of these instructions precisely will result in the officer determining that they have observed clues.

As previously mentioned, if the officer observes enough "clues" during any of the tests, then they can, and typically will place the subject under arrest for DWI. At that point, the officer informs the driver that they are being arrested for suspicion of operating a motor vehicle while intoxicated and requests that the driver provide a sample of their breath or blood for alcohol testing.

If the subject consents to provide a specimen, then they will provide a breath sample by blowing into a machine or will have their blood drawn at a hospital or the police station. If the subject refuses to provide a breath or blood specimen, then the officer can choose to request a warrant from a judge to have a sample of blood taken. Eventually, the subject will receive a bond amount and hopefully be able to bond out of jail; this is when the real process begins.

CHAPTER 2

IS SOMEONE REQUIRED TO SUBMIT TO SFSTS OR ALCOHOL TESTING IN TEXAS?

The short answer is no, however, every decision has a consequence.

A refusal to consent to a blood or breath test can result in the suspension of a person's driver's license. It is possible to contest that suspension and keep it from being suspended in a proceeding called Administrative License Review or ALR. This is a great opportunity for a defense attorney to get evidence early and begin planning the defense.

Roadside breath tests, often referred to as portable breath tests (PBT), are not admissible in court, and they are not used very often in Texas. An individual is not required to consent to a PBT and will not have any license suspension consequences as a result of this specific refusal.

Refusal to submit to the field sobriety tests (SFSTs) does not result in additional license suspension consequences. But the truth of the matter is, if it got to the point where an officer has requested a driver to perform the sobriety tests, then they have probably already decided to arrest the suspect for DWI regardless of how a suspect performs. Therefore you must ask yourself, is there a good reason to voluntarily give the officer potential additional evidence?

It is not difficult to explain to a jury the many factors which could explain why a person might not perform well on the roadside standardized field sobriety tests.

CHAPTER 3

THE DRIVER'S LICENSE CONSEQUENCES ASSOCIATED WITH A DWI ARREST AND CONVICTION

If a person refuses to provide a breath or blood sample upon request, then their driver's license will be automatically suspended. If a person does provide a breath or blood sample and they are shown to have a blood alcohol concentration of 0.08 or higher, then their driver's license will be suspended. The breath test results are immediate; within seconds of providing a breath sample, the result will be available, and the person's license could be suspended at that point. A blood sample, on the other hand, must be sent to the DPS crime lab for analysis, which takes time. The driver's license will not be suspended during the interim.

Why Are The Days Following A DWI Charge So Critical For A Driver's License In Texas?

A driver's license suspension for a refusal to provide a breath or blood sample is theoretically automatic, however, a person has 15 days from the date they receive the notice of the suspension and the corresponding paperwork to have their attorney request an administrative license review (ALR) hearing to challenge the driver's license suspension.

It is important to hire an attorney as quickly as possible because if that 15-day window is missed, the opportunity to challenge the suspension will have been lost. Challenging the license suspension is something we do in every DWI case because it gives us an early opportunity to get some of the evidence—perhaps even before the prosecutor does. It also gives us an opportunity to win the hearing and ensure that the client can keep their license.

Is There Anything Available For People Charged With DWI In Texas To Be Allowed To Drive During A Period Of Suspension?

Individuals who have had their driver's license suspended because of a breath or blood test refusal, or as a result of a conviction are eligible for what is called an occupational driver's license. The purpose of this type of license is to allow a person to be able to drive a vehicle for things like work or medical appointments. This type of license comes with restrictions and conditions, such as geographical and time restrictions, as well as the possible requirement of an ignition interlock device in the vehicle. However, many of these restrictions and conditions can be negotiated with the prosecutor. For example, if the defendant lives in Galveston but works in Houston, then it would be possible to ensure that the geographical restrictions on the occupational license do not prohibit them from traveling to and from their place of work.

Most first time DWI offenders are eligible for an occupational license without having a waiting period. However, if an individual has prior DWI history there is a potential that person will have to wait a period of up to 180 days before they can apply for this type of license. A knowledgeable attorney can help can guide someone through the entire process to ensure that they have the ability to drive as soon as possible.

CHAPTER 4

THE AGGRAVATING FACTORS FOR DWI CHARGES IN TEXAS

There is a multitude of factors that can aggravate a DWI. Primarily the factors fall into two different categories: statutory, those prescribed by law, and non-statutory, those that make the offense optically worse but do not add any additional legal penalty.

Aggravating statutory factors elevate the level of offense and increase the punishment range, and in some instances making the offense a felony. The most common statutory aggravating factors are prior DWI convictions. Each prior conviction (even if it did not occur in the State of Texas) will elevate the punishment range and degree of the offense.

A first-time DWI is a Class B misdemeanor, which is punishable by up to 180 days in the county jail and a maximum fine of $2,000. A second DWI is a Class A misdemeanor, which is punishable by up to 365 days in jail and a maximum fine of $4,000. A third DWI is a third-degree felony, which is punishable by two to 10 years in prison in the Institutional Division of the Texas Department of Criminal Justice and a maximum fine of $10,000. In addition to the fines, there is also an annual fee of up to $2,000 for three years to retain an individual's driver's license.

However, the presence of certain facts in the case can trigger an enhanced degree of offense and punishment range as a matter of law even if it is a first-time offense. For example, if it is found that the individual accused has a blood alcohol concentration of 0.15 or more, the degree of the offense can be increased from a Class B misdemeanor to a Class A misdemeanor. For another example, if there is a child under the age of 15 present in the vehicle the degree of offense can be increased to a state jail felony, which is punishable by not less than 6 months and up to 2 years in the state jail division of the Texas Department of Criminal Justice and a fine not to exceed $10,000. Additionally, DWIs where there is an accident that results in serious bodily injury and/or death have entirely different classifications, degrees, punishment ranges, and aggravating factors.

Non-statutory aggravating factors do not come with an increased degree of offense or punishment range but can cause a prosecutor to push for harsher punishments than they otherwise would in the absence of such factors. Examples of these types of factors include poor driving facts such as driving well in excess of the speed limit or driving in such an egregious manner that places the public in danger. The occurrence of an accident is can also have the same effect, even if no one was injured.

What Are The Typical Penalties For A First-Time And Subsequent DWI Conviction In Texas?

There is no typical sentence for a DWI in Texas because there are simply too many varying factors that come into play. Aggravating factors can greatly affect the penalties for a DWI charge, and there are many different types of aggravating factors. However, it can be said that jail time is unlikely for a first-time DWI, although it is still a real possibility. In lieu of jail, there may be different types of probation for this type of offense. Additionally, in many counties throughout Texas, there are pre-trial intervention programs for first-time DWI offenders who have no criminal history. The program is similar to probation, but once the term has been finished, the DWI case will be dismissed.

Another consideration when assessing the potential punishment outcome of a DWI offense is the local customs for the courts where a person's case may land. For example, one judge might say that a first-time DWI with a blood alcohol content of less than 0.15 does not call for serious punishment, but that a blood alcohol content above 0.15 should result in a specific punishment.

As another example, a judge in felony court might only grant probation under very limited circumstances. It is critically important to have an attorney very familiar with the attitudes and customs of the courts in order to plan a strategic defense to a DWI case.

Do You Recommend Pre-Trial Voluntary Counseling For Your Clients In DWI Cases?

If a client believes that they have a problem with alcohol, then I might encourage them to seek pre-trial counseling. This would not only be in the best interests of the client but also allow us to show the prosecutor that the client is being proactive in handling their issue. However, it is often the case that a defendant does not have a problem that needs to be addressed. For example, someone who simply had a glass of wine with dinner could end up getting arrested for DWI. Ultimately, it is up to the client to decide whether to seek pre-trial counseling.

CHAPTER 5

HOW MUCH WILL A PRIOR DWI ARREST OR CONVICTION IMPACT MY DWI CASE?

In general, prior DWI convictions increase the punishment range of the immediate DWI charge. If someone has a prior DWI conviction, the degree of offense can increase depending on how many prior convictions.

The State will have to be able to prove these prior convictions in order to use them for enhancement purposes. A skilled attorney will evaluate the State's evidence of prior convictions and determine whether the State will be able to prove them. This little detail alone can drastically change the outcome of a pending DWI.

Apart from the effect of prior DWI convictions and enhancements, there are other factors related to previous DWI convictions that can have an impact on things like potential plea negotiations. For example, the amount of time that has elapsed between a previous conviction and the current DWI charge can make a significant difference in the outcome of the new case. If a prior DWI conviction occurred 10 years prior, then it will not have as much of an impact as a previous conviction that is very close in time to the new DWI charge. The current DWI likely still be enhanced to a 2nd or 3rd DWI, but the punishment options that the State is willing to offer will be affected and could be the difference between probation and jail time.

A prior criminal history that's not related to DWI will not necessarily impact the DWI case. However, it would be considered during negotiations of a sentence in plea bargaining. For example, a person who was released from the penitentiary for a felony offense just prior to getting a DWI will be treated more harshly than a client who has never before been arrested. Although a prosecutor is supposed to only look at the case before them, it's impossible to take a prior DWI out of one's mind. It can—and I would argue that it often does—influence the way a case is presented and tried.

CHAPTER 6

POTENTIAL DEFENSES THAT WE USE TO DEFEND CLIENTS FACING DWI CHARGES

DWI defense of all types is very technical and complex in nature. It requires a thorough examination of many intricacies, rules, and regulations that must be adhered to by law enforcement. Our analysis of a case starts with the initial stop. Specifically, we must consider whether the stop was legal. If the officer's stop is not legal then it could lead to the exclusion of evidence and ultimately dismissal.

Assuming the officer's stop was valid, we then analyze the officer's investigation. This involves determining whether the officer had sufficient reasonable suspicion to detain the suspect for further DWI investigation. If it appears that the officer did have sufficient probable cause, then we analyze the way in which the officer conducted the SFSTs. There are very specific rules for how the officer must conduct these tests and an officer should have continual training in this area.

Additionally, we will also need to verify the validity of the breath or blood test conducted—especially if video footage shows no evidence of intoxication, but the breath or blood test does. If a breath test was conducted, we will determine the date of the last calibration of the machine that was used. A similar investigation will be done to determine whether a blood sample was properly handled, stored, and tested. I once handled a case wherein I discovered that the officer drove around with the blood sample in the trunk of the vehicle for one week before turning it in for testing.

Even in cases where the evidence seems stacked against the client, it may very well be the case that the procedures or tests were mishandled, which could result in a desirable outcome for the client. Anyone who is facing a DWI conviction should have their case investigated by a lawyer. Even if a suitable defense cannot be found, a lawyer can still negotiate to have the consequences mitigated as much as possible.

CHAPTER 7

HOW WOULD YOU ADVISE A CLIENT WHO WANTS TO PLEAD GUILTY TO DWI CHARGES?

When a client wants to just throw in the towel and plead guilty to a DWI charge, I encourage them to allow me to do my job. I tell them that unless I am able to launch an investigation, we'll never know how the case could have turned out. For example, showing that a sample of blood was stored improperly could lead to a successful motion to suppress evidence, which could result in the dismissal of the case. There is too much at stake in a DWI case to plead guilty before an investigation has been done.

The collateral consequences of a DWI conviction include a driver's license suspension, which could have negative impacts on employment opportunities or even the loss of a job. Obviously, any term of incarceration can be problematic. Even a misdemeanor DWI charge can result in a 30-day jail sentence. Many prosecutors act like a sentence of only 30 days is not a big deal, so I have to explain to them that when a person's livelihood is taken away for 30 days, they lose the ability to pay their mortgage and bills and to take care of their children and animals. In my opinion, even a very small amount of jail time can have a big impact on a person's life.

Probation is a punishment that is not meant to be convenient. Probation officers generally don't coddle their probationers, and most probationers will get the feeling that their probation officers are mean. The conditions of probation generally include paying fines, community service, and paying a fee to the state of Texas in order to maintain a driver's license.

DWI is a unique crime in that it is not what I would consider it being an intentional crime. While someone who decides to rob an establishment clearly has the intention to commit a crime, most people who get charged with DWI do not think that they were intoxicated and didn't intend to commit a crime. With so many possible collateral consequences and potentially devastating consequences, there is simply too much at stake to plead guilty before having a lawyer conduct a thorough analysis of the case.

CHAPTER 8

IS IT POSSIBLE TO HAVE A DWI CASE REMOVED FROM MY RECORD?

Whether a DWI can be removed from an individual's criminal history depends entirely on the final resolution of the case. Was the case dismissed? Was the individual given probation? What type of probation? The answers to these questions determine whether all or part, of the charge, can be removed from an individual's criminal history. The laws regarding this are very strict and attempts to have them removed are often challenged by the Texas Department of Public Safety.

There are two mechanisms that keep an arrest or charges off of a person's criminal record: expunction and non-disclosure. An expunction is a mechanism that erases all records of an arrest or charges from an individual's criminal history making it as if it never happened. A person who has been charged with a DWI offense will only be eligible for an expunction if the case is outright dismissed for evidentiary reasons, if the individual successfully completed a pre-trial intervention program, or if at trial a jury rendered a verdict of not guilty.

However, due to a 2019 legislative change that amended the punishments available for DWIs non-disclosures are now possible for certain qualified individuals. A non-disclosure removes the record of the offense from an individual's criminal history available to the public. Law enforcement and government agencies will still be able to see the offense on the record, but potential public employers and the like conducting background checks would not. This was made possible because the legislative change created the option of deferred adjudication as a possible punishment for first-time offenses. If a person successfully completes the terms of deferred adjudication, the case will not result in a final conviction and the individual will be eligible for a non-disclosure.

Some counties have what are called pre-trial diversion/intervention programs. The terms and conditions, and who may qualify for these programs vary from county to county. Essentially, however, these programs function just like probation or deferred adjudication with the only difference being the final outcome of the case upon the successful completion of the program. For pre-trial diversion/intervention programs, the case will be dismissed after completion and are often eligible for an expunction or non-disclosure.

CHAPTER 9

HIRING A LAWYER TO HAVE THE BEST POSSIBLE DEFENSE IN TEXAS

Everyone deserves the best possible defense because no matter what, a conviction follows a person for life. If someone gets convicted today and receives a DWI 10 years from now, then it will be considered a second DWI. It's important to have a lawyer ensure that the state meets its burden of proof in getting a conviction, and if the state cannot meet this burden, then there needs to be a lawyer there to expose that and get the case dismissed or get a not guilty verdict from a jury.

DWI defense is a very challenging area of the law that requires constant education, learning, reading, and attendance at seminars to stay current on the latest science; this is critical to building the best defense for every client. Over the course of 22 years in DWI law, I can attest to the many changes that have occurred, such as the implementation of breath and blood tests, dash and body cams, and field sobriety tests. As technology has advanced, so too has the amount of evidence, but this brings up new challenges for which every DWI lawyer must be on the lookout. For example, I handled a case wherein the officer turned off his body cam to say, "I don't actually think this person is intoxicated," and then turned the body camera back on. I was able to discover this because the other officer who was standing right beside him did not turn off the sound on his body camera.

There are so many nuances and technical issues in every DWI case that can entirely change the outcome. It's critical to have a lawyer who has been trained in DWI defense and has the experience to identify problems in the state's case; without the right knowledge and experience, these problems can go unnoticed like a needle in a haystack.

INDEX

N

O

P

R

S

T

V

W

NOTES

Made in the USA
Monee, IL
05 November 2026

67385070R00033